A PORTFOLIO OF

WATER GARDEN & SPECIALTY LANDSCAPE IDEAS

CONTENTS

**What Makes a Great Water Garden
or Specialty Landscape?** 5

Planning 7

    Evaluate the Situation 7

    Function & Features 8

    Adding Value 10

Specialty Features 14

    Elements of Landscape Design 14

    Working With Water 17

    Retaining Walls 20

    Arbors, Fences & Pergolas 24

    Gazebos & Garden Houses 28

    Porches, Patios & Decks 32

Managing Movement 38

    Paths & Walkways 38

    Bridges & Steps 40

Types of Gardens 43

    Great Garden Ideas 43

    Flower Gardens 44

    Shade & Vegetable Gardens 46

    Container & Sculpture Gardens 48

A Portfolio of Water Garden & Specialty Landscape Ideas 50

Water Gardens 52

Theme Gardens 64

Backyard Sanctuary 74

Visual Impressions 84

List of Contributors 96

712
Landscape

© Copyright 1996
Cy DeCosse Incorporated
5900 Green Oak Drive
Minnetonka, Minnesota 55343
1-800-328-3895
All rights reserved

Printed in Hong Kong
Library of Congress
Cataloging-in-Publication Data
A Portfolio of Water Garden & Specialty Landscape Ideas
p. cm.

ISBN 0-86573-975-7 (softcover)
1. Water in landscape architecture. 2. Gardens—Design.
3. Garden ornaments and furniture. 4. Water gardens.
I. Cy DeCosse Incorporated.
SB475.8.P67 1996
712—dc20
95-44655

Author: Home How-To Institute™
Creative Director: William B. Jones
Associate Creative Director: Tim Himsel
Group Executive Editor: Paul Currie
Managing Editor: Carol Harvatin
Editor: Mark Biscan
Art Director: Gina Seeling
Copy Editor: Janice Cauley
Vice President of Development
    Planning & Production: Jim Bindas
Production Coordinator: Laura Hokkanen

Printed by Shiny International (0296)

CY DECOSSE INCORPORATED

A COWLES MAGAZINES COMPANY

Chairman/CEO: Bruce Barnet
Chairman Emeritus: Cy DeCosse
President & Chief Operating Officer: Nino Tarantino
Editor-in-Chief: William B. Jones

(above) **A unique backyard setting is** created using free-form cement patio slabs, modeled to look like natural stone. A simple wooden bridge spans a small man-made creek and unites the flat backyard area with a sloping hillside.

(right) **A feature fountain** is the centerpiece of this garden pond area. The fountain not only adds a lovely visual effect, it also creates the soothing sound of moving water.

WHAT MAKES A GREAT WATER GARDEN OR SPECIALTY LANDSCAPE?

Every yard or outdoor environment is unique. Depending on the physical characteristics of the land, the function you wish your outdoor space to provide and the types of elements you wish to include, you can create a specialized landscape that includes a water garden, as well as other specialty landscape features.

There are a number of exciting and effective ways to create a specialty landscape almost anywhere. Your landscape should unite all elements and structures into one harmonious whole. From enhancing a deck with small container gardens to coordinating an entire water garden setting, complete with gazebo and ornamental sculpture garden, the range of options is almost limitless.

Water gardens and other water elements are one of the most popular ways to create a special spot within a landscape. With new materials and building techniques a pond can be built on a small scale for a reasonable cost.

Other popular landscape elements you might want to consider adding to a specialty landscape design include a recreation area, such as a deck or patio, a path or walkway, or a decorative fence. Also consider functional uses for plants, trees and shrubs as windbreaks, noise buffers and substitutes for the usual lawn grass in a yard design.

A well-designed landscape allows your family to enjoy a variety of activities at one time. An example of a multifunctional yard may include: play spaces for children, gardening areas for the family gardener, a patio with a cooking area for entertaining and relaxing and a garden pond for quiet contemplation.

This well-orchestrated landscape incorporates a variety of coordinated planting areas with an attractive open-weave fence, a small, raised planting bed, a brick walkway and other elements throughout the yard.

(right) ***A rustic brick patio*** *features an open area for dining and entertaining. An arbor and white lattice wall create an intimate sitting area on one end of the patio. A small garden wall, filled with a variety of flowering plants, borders the patio and separates it from the open lawn on the other side of the wall.*

(below) ***A sunny hillside patio*** *features a garden pond constructed from natural stone. A beautiful teak furniture grouping creates a cozy corner for conversation or quiet pondside meditation.*

Planning
EVALUATE THE SITUATION

Although the exterior design of your home might be conducive to a specific type of desired landscape feature, the actual physical characteristics of the land will determine what elements can be used. This is why it's best to begin with your existing site and develop a plan for an outdoor area that can be created within the perimeters of your space.

Consider how your outdoor area will be used. How does your family spend time when outdoors? An intimate water garden might be just the thing for someone seeking a quiet sanctuary or wildlife habitat. For others, a large poolside patio or deck would do better to satisfy the desire for an outdoor area for activities such as swimming or sunbathing. Researching the many options available will help you design an outdoor environment with specialty elements and features that will satisfy everyone's outdoor needs.

When attempting to make the maximum use of your outdoor space you may be faced with a number of common problems, such as trying to create a space large enough, in a small outdoor area, to entertain a number of people. On the other hand, if you have a large sprawling outdoor space you may want to make it more intimate, or break the space into separate activity areas.

Start with a rough drawing of your lot, and include all assets and problem areas as you see them. When analyzing your lot, include: the direction of winds; the direction and angle of the sun at various times of the day; and any unsightly views from your yard, such as a building or vacant lot. Also include assets you wish to accentuate, such as mature trees and a pleasant view.

Photo courtesy of Sticks and Stones Innovative Decks and Landscape Design

A small backyard landscape has been carefully planned and executed to create the feel of a much larger formal garden. Effective use of space creates several activity areas and makes the most out of every inch in this multifunctional landscape masterpiece.

Decorative outdoor lighting adds an interesting aesthetic feature. The attractive light fixtures illuminate a stone path that winds through the garden and guide users safely through the garden at night.

Planning
FUNCTION & FEATURES

Gardens are for plants and yards are for people; they each serve very different functions. Yards are very versatile and can be used for a number of different functions from lawn games, such as badminton or croquet, to a family barbecue. These areas can hardly be called gardens, so the term lawn is used. An outdoor space may include a garden, perhaps with a theme, such as a water garden or sculpture garden.

Adding water in the form of a fountain, fish pond or water garden brings tranquility to a busy landscape. Freshwater clams, snails and underwater oxygenating plants keep the water clear and the algae away, creating an ecologically balanced environment.

Many specialty landscape features are multifunctional, such as raised flower beds, retaining walls and low railings, which can be used for extra seating. Fences, arbors and pergolas provide protection from sun and wind, as well as a place for hanging plants, not to mention the interesting visual appeal these structures bring to an outdoor setting. Other landscape elements such as decks, porches and patios are versatile indoor-outdoor spaces that are easily accessible from many areas of the house and yard. They can be used for a variety of activities from personal relaxation to sunbathing to family gatherings.

Repeating materials, design motifs and finishes throughout a landscape unifies the overall look. Outdoor lighting is another way to bring the elements of an outdoor area together. There are several types of outdoor lighting features that can be used to add safety as well as dramatic accents to a landscape. They make the yard interesting and inviting at night. Lighting fixtures are designed to inconspicuously blend into the landscape during the day and come to life at night illuminating steps, changes in the terrain, a driveway entrance or an interesting feature in the yard.

(left) **To get back to nature** a small backyard is transformed into a natural woodland setting, complete with a stream and footbridge. A tall fence encloses the space and keeps it private and secluded.

(below) **This flower gardener's landscape** is alive with color. Several planting beds overflow with flowers, including the flat, level areas of a terraced retaining wall. A wooden arbor adds an interesting accent and a place for hanging plants.

*This **simple landscape** uses a combination of plants and materials to create a beautiful balance of color and texture.*

Planning
ADDING VALUE

The first impression people have of your home is greatly influenced by the landscaping that surrounds it. A landscape should enhance the outside of a house, not overpower or overshadow it. A well-kept landscape, with mature trees and plantings, is a sure way to add value and curb appeal to any home.

Trees are one of the most valuable additions

Small trees and shrubs *soften the transition from the house to the ground. Even a modest landscape adds instant curb appeal to a home.*

you can make to a yard. Deciduous trees, such as Japanese maples and crab apples add scale and cool shade to a yard. Evergreens, such as cedars, provide a year-round windbreak.

Color comes from flowering plants that are interspersed around them. Foliage plays an important part in the color and texture of the garden as well as the overall look. When adding bushes or small trees to your landscape avoid monotonous, uniform planting patterns, and be careful not to locate shrubs where they will grow to block views from windows.

A great landscape plan adds value by accentuating the most prominent features of your yard, and creating a natural setting that allows your house to become a part of the landscape.

Many specialty features, such as paths, bridges, fences, walls, gazebos and arbors are decorative elements that also perform an important function within the landscape. Elements like benches and seats offer a place for garden users to sit quietly and enjoy the garden.

Gazebos, garden houses, arbors, pergolas and trellises are structures that will bring protection from the elements to the setting. They also have a strong visual impact because they are so noticeable in most outdoor settings.

Try to combine complementary accents for your outdoor area and place them so they showcase other landscape elements in the best possible setting. Plants and structural elements should complement and enhance each other.

The classic style of this English Tudor home is complemented by a raised circular planting bed made of the same natural stone as seen in the house. Low bushes, mixed with colorful patches of flowers, line the foundation and soften the transition from hard stone to the soft green lawn.

ADDING VALUE

Plants around a house can serve many different purposes; they help soften, cool, screen and define an outdoor area. Your landscape design also brings you the satisfaction of expressing a personal style. Trees and shrubs can be used to enhance the view of your home, or they can block one that's not so pleasant. Landscape plantings help soften the hard lines created by the corners and walls of a house, and other hard landscape elements, such as patios, decks and the hard edges of a rock or cement water garden or pond. Surrounding trees provide shade and protection from the hot sun and chilling winds.

Because the trees and shrubs you plant along your foundation will be permanent, careful selection is necessary. The types of plants you select will affect the amount of maintenance and overall look of your home. Different plants will have different effects. They differ in texture, color,

form and size. Plants are valuable assets for more than decorative reasons; they offer a variety of practical assets as well. They offer a screen for privacy or shade; they can reduce maintenance areas; they can define different areas in the outdoor space.

Remember to choose plants whose color coordinates with the exterior of your home as well as the surrounding foliage. New trees should be planted so they will frame the house as they mature. Select plants that will stay in scale with the architectural features of your house when they are full grown.

Trees can be strategically planted to provide a windbreak from chilling winter winds, which helps conserve heat and reduces snowdrifts. When planting a landscape for a new home, position one or two fast-growing trees near the corners of the house and slower-growing trees on the other corners and along the back.

(below) **Crab apples** *are an excellent choice for a small flowering tree you can use in a garden. They add exceptional beauty and form all year round. Throughout the summer they add shade and beauty. Their fruits add interest in the late summer and fall.*

Crab apples are available in a variety of shapes and sizes *that will complement any garden design, ranging from small and shrublike, to tall and spreading.*

Mature trees, such as the birch and evergreen trees in this yard, are a welcome addition to any landscape. They bring shade, visually appealing shapes and textures, and colorful foliage, to any yard.

ELEMENTS OF LANDSCAPE DESIGN

There are essentially two ways to enhance a landscape or water garden setting; one is with plantings, and the other is with structural elements. Take into consideration the exterior style, proportion and size of your house when deciding on what types of elements and structures to include in your landscape or water garden design.

A water feature is a garden accent that is increasing in popularity. New developments in liners makes a water garden an option for almost every type of landscape or outdoor setting. With so many options available today a water garden can be anything from a small pool to a wall of cascading water that adds great visual interest and the pleasant sound of splashing water. The still water of ponds and pools has a beautiful reflective quality that is enhanced even more when combined with specialty lighting for an incredible nightscape quality.

Moving water can be either broken or unbroken. An unbroken waterscape includes water that falls in uninterrupted sheets or uninterrupted streams. In a water garden that has broken cascades, the fall is broken by boulders and rock ledges that direct the flow. Broken falls look the more natural and often have several tiers.

The structural, or hardscape, elements of a landscape have as much influence on an outdoor setting as the plants. They provide focal points throughout a landscape, guide users around an outdoor setting and offer shelter and comfortable seating for those who wish to linger in the outdoors for long periods of time.

Trellises, arbors, pergolas, fences, gazebos and garden houses are specialty garden structures that give an outdoor setting special charm. They are both decorative and functional, and make a pleasing focal point nestled within a lush green garden, or on a rolling green lawn. Specialty garden structures provide shade, privacy, support for plants and a sense of enclosure and protection in an outdoor setting.

Plants, such as climbing vines and flowering annuals, are a colorful way to put the finishing touches on any of these specialty structures. Adding plants to a landscape also adds privacy, color and fragrance.

Specialty landscape structures *add a dimension of aesthetic decoration to your garden. They are a way of introducing stone, wood and other landscape materials as design elements to your landscape.*

Photo courtesy of Champlain Stone, Ltd.

A beautiful, natural stone retaining wall acts as a dramatic backdrop for this formal poolside patio. The expansive wall makes usable space out of a barren hillside. The same natural stone used in the wall is used to accent the edge of the pool and continue the design theme throughout.

The curved shape of this swimming pool coordinates well with the irregular shapes of the cut stone patio. Stepping stones and irregular flagstones lead to the pool area, where a well-manicured planting area creates a small formal garden, poolside.

(below) **A small creek** brings the unique element of moving water to this backyard setting.

WORKING WITH WATER

Pools can have two meanings when you are talking about using them in a landscape design. In gardens, a pool usually means a decorative pool or pond, whereas in the yard one usually thinks of a place for swimming and sunning. Pools are usually integrated with a deck or patio that is connected with the house. Hot tubs and spas are popular places for people to gather in an outdoor setting. The materials around them should be skidproof and comfortable to bare feet. Some good choices are redwood, tile, slate, flagstone, brick or concrete.

Furniture, flowers and planting containers are just a few of the ways you can dress up and accent an outdoor pool area with a splash of color. Incorporating the swimming pool into the landscape includes positioning the pool so it is hit by as much sunlight as possible. Screens, fences, walls and hedges add protection from the wind as well as privacy.

One way to incorporate a swimming pool into the landscape plan is to make it a featured element of the yard and use a common element, such as flagstone, as a border to create a uniform feel to the entire setting.

Some pools have an adjacent spa connected to them to help relax away the tensions of a busy day. Others have a realistic free-form shape and are surrounded by natural features, such as boulders, to help create the illusion of a realistic pond. You may choose to include a waterfall or stream that cascades into the pool for a stunning effect. Boulders placed around the edges of the pool create an authentic woodland feeling.

Photo courtesy of Buechel Stone Corp of Chilton and Fon du lac, Wisconsin

*A **large, inviting stone patio** surrounds this backyard pool and offers plenty of room for poolside activities. Even when not in use, the tranquil beauty of the rippling water adds an element of movement to the setting.*

WORKING WITH WATER

Garden pools can have a formal or an informal look depending on the materials and shapes you decide to use. Pools with a rigid geometric shape, such as a square or rectangle, have a formal look, while those with a free-form shape, similar to the contours of a natural pond, create a much more casual atmosphere. Fountains, statues and waterfalls are other elements that add a formal feel to a water garden.

Informal water gardens recreate the shape and appearance of a natural pond, including the plants found in a natural water habitat. These types of gardens require a delicate combination of plant types and animal life to achieve a harmonious environment. The balance is achieved by using the right plant species with the appropriate number and types of animal life.

Water lilies and lotus are bold, beautiful plants most often associated with flowering water gardens. They keep the water cool, replenish the oxygen and provide a haven for fish. Oxygenating plants, such as submerged grasses, keep the water clean by keeping down the algae growth. They also provide food and shelter for fish.

Certain types of water plants, known as bog plants, create a natural border around the edge of a pond. These plants grow in the shallow areas of a pond and their leaves and flowers can be seen above the water's surface. Some common varieties of this type include cattails, water irises and water poppies. Another type of water plant, such as water chestnuts, floats on the water's surface and also helps control algae growth.

Photo courtesy of Cy DeCosse Inc.

*A **small fountain**, in the center of this garden pond, adds the lively sound of moving water. The surrounding plants work well in this informal setting and blend with the natural environment.*

Photo courtesy of Featherock, Incorporated

(left) **The compelling sound** and movement of cascading water adds a special touch to any water garden setting.

(below) **A small, shallow pool** is the focal point of this formal garden. The statue in the center adds an artistic element to the setting. An open-sided, Victorian gazebo provides a quiet corner to sit and enjoy this elegant garden.

Photo courtesy of Gazebo Central

19

Specialty Features
RETAINING WALLS

One of the first steps in creating your outdoor environment is to define the boundaries of the space. One way to do this is to add a perimeter wall either on the property line or as the boundary of the yard.

Retaining walls are barriers that hold earth in place and help ease the transition from one level to another in an outdoor environment. A series of low retaining walls is one way to shape a sloping, hilly lot and turn an unusable hillside into a series of manageable, level areas.

Besides the functional value a retaining wall adds to a landscape, it also has an aesthetic impact on a landscape. You can use a retaining wall to enclose a patio and create seating at the same time. Low retaining walls can also be used as raised planting beds. The descending levels can be planted a number of ways to add an interesting visual to any landscape. A raised planting bed is easier to tend than one located on ground level.

A large retaining wall was built into a steep hillside to make an effective sunny beach area. The different levels create areas for sunbathing and social gatherings, as well as areas for landscaping with shrubs and other plants.

*The **natural look** of an interlocking block retaining wall blends beautifully with the natural flagstone steps and walkway. The various planting areas created by the wall give this landscape a formal feel and reduce the amount of yard maintenance.*

RETAINING WALLS

Wide steps can also serve as retaining walls that connect one area of the yard with another. You can create an interesting landscape feature on a steep slope by alternating short retaining walls with steps as they descend the slope. Retaining walls can also add an interesting change in elevation to a flat, uninteresting yard. Wall/step combinations create terraced areas that can be landscaped many different ways. Low-maintenance plantings add a finishing touch to a retaining wall and soften its hard edges. The flowers you choose should be proportional to the size and style of the retaining wall and complement the surrounding landscape.

The material you choose, and the type of wall, will influence the feel of the outdoor setting you wish to create. The most commonly used materials for retaining walls include brick, wood and stone. When choosing materials for your retaining wall consider how the wall will be used and how strong it needs to be, depending on how much earth it will have to hold back. Retaining walls more than three feet high require a foundation.

Drainage is also a critical concern with retaining walls. Heavy rains and melting snow saturate the earth, and while flowing downhill they exert so much pressure on a wall there is a chance it will be demolished if the water is not allowed to run off through weep holes created at strategic points along the wall to relieve pressure. You may want to consult a professional landscaper when building retaining walls.

(above) ***A large, multitiered retaining wall*** *helps manage the steep hillside by creating level areas that can be used for planting beds or left as open lawn area.*

((left) **The rustic look** *of an English countryside is the effect this fieldstone retaining wall evokes. A mixture of flowering plants, shrubs and small trees soften the hard feel of the stone.*

(bottom left) **An interlocking brick wall** *carries the formal look of the landscape to the next level of this lawn.*

(bottom right) **A decorative retaining wall** *combines form with function by creating multilevel planting areas that are filled with colorful blooming plants.*

ARBORS, FENCES & PERGOLAS

Arbors, and their vertical counterparts, trellises, are a decorative way to bring shade to a sunny spot in your yard or garden. They act as open walls that define an area without enclosing it. Arbors and trellises are usually made of thin, narrow pieces of lath that are nailed together in a diamond or square pattern. The open-weave design of arbors, pergolas and some fences can be used as a support for climbing plants. New on the market are lattice products made from durable vinyl. They offer the look of a painted wood lattice, but they don't need painting and are very resistant to wear and aging.

Arbors can be used as a focal point in any garden setting. They can be used to make an inviting entryway to a garden area, as a frame for a special view or to make a transition from one area of the yard to another. Arbors are a charming way to add shade to a sunny spot in the yard.

The crisp white, open-weave design of this arbor and trellis wall gives this setting a delicate appeal. The open lattice design of the wall provides a place for climbing vines.

A redwood pergola, *painted classic white, draws the focus to the gate in this charming country garden. A matching fence encloses the yard and carries the design throughout.*

ARBORS, FENCES & PERGOLAS

Arbors, fences and pergolas are charming landscape structures that bring shade to any sunny spot in the yard. Arbors, fences and pergolas can be built of many materials, from cedar and redwood to brick and stone. Even bamboo can be used to create an interesting focal point in a garden setting.

An overhead arbor or pergola makes an inviting entryway to a garden area, or a frame for a special view. These structures can also be used to indicate a transition from one area of the yard to another. Fences define the boundaries of a garden area and provide privacy and protection from the elements.

Originally from Italy, pergolas were designed as structures to grow vines and ripen grapes on. Pergolas create a covered walkway that encourages garden users to walk beneath. They are perfect for shading walkways and paths that connect one area of the yard with another. The placement of a pergola is important, because it needs a destination on the other side, such as a gazebo or garden pond, where pergola users end up. A pergola without a destination or a definite beginning or end, is simply an arbor.

Arbors add a romantic quality to a garden. Even a plain arbor creates a dramatic effect when decorated with colorful climbing plants. An arbor should blend with the rest of the outdoor space in style and size. Fences can be constructed from a combination of different materials to create an interesting effect, such as brick posts with wooden panels. Fences that include an open lattice pattern have a lighter feel. The open pattern makes the structure seem less imposing and lets in a bit of the view from the other side.

A tall redwood fence brings privacy and seclusion to this outdoor area. An ornate overhead pergola draws attention to the entrance and guides users through the large double gate.

Photo courtesy of California Redwood Association

Photo courtesy of California Redwood Association

(right) **A beautiful redwood pergola** *separates one area of this landscape from another without using a solid barrier. The pergola frames the view looking out from the top of the steps.*

(above) **An elaborate version** *of the classic white picket fence adds a charming traditional touch to an otherwise simple house. The rustic stone wall carries the traditional quality throughout the yard.*

27

Specialty Features
GAZEBOS & GARDEN HOUSES

Gazebos and garden houses are another type of decorative garden structure that adds character to any garden and can be enjoyed all year long. They are a charming way to provide shelter in a garden. They offer the same kind of open-air charm as an arbor or pergola, but with more protection from the elements. Gazebos are usually freestanding structures with open-air sides, which are sometimes screened, and solid roofs and floors. The variety of designs for these elements is very diverse, ranging from a simple structure consisting of an open roof over a sitting area to an elaborately detailed structure with built-in benches and ornate railings.

A Victorian-style gazebo adds an old-fashioned charm to this woodland setting. An antique carousel horse helps capture the feel of another era.

Photos both pages courtesy of CROSS VINYLattice Atlanta, GA

A grand Victorian-style gazebo adds an element of architectural interest to an outdoor setting and provides a sheltered spot to sit and enjoy the view. This large gazebo sits atop a garden wall, overlooking the swimming pool and four poolside fountains. The sight and sound of the cascading water is a point of interest for those in the pool, as well as those sitting in the gazebo.

GAZEBOS & GARDEN HOUSES

Placement, size, design, use and budget are the most important factors to consider when planning and designing your gazebo or garden house. The gazebo or garden house you choose should blend well with the design style of your house, as well as other structural elements in your yard, to maintain a consistency throughout the landscape. You can also establish consistency by using the same colors and materials throughout the construction of all your specialty landscape structures.

This inspired gazebo design came from combining two arched arbors and connecting them at the top. The arches add the perception of enclosing the space, while the open sides allow users to enjoy the fresh air and outdoor environment from this comfortable alcove.

A screened-in gazebo creates an outdoor haven from biting insects. This roomy outdoor structure provides a private sanctuary for recreation and relaxation.

The elaborate elegance of this gazebo is enhanced beautifully by the reflective quality of the water. The curved roof and scalloped valances, featured as part of the open walls, match the detail in the railings.

PORCHES, PATIOS & DECKS

Porches, patios and decks offer effective solutions to increasing your outdoor living space and reducing the amount of maintenance your yard requires. Decks, porches and patios are constructed of all-weather materials and provide a solid, level surface for people, furniture, planting containers and other outdoor accessories.

A porch is a welcome haven from rain and snow as well as a handy place to remove and leave wet boots, raincoats and umbrellas. Screened-in porches are especially popular where insects are a problem. Decks are especially effective at creating usable space out of a steep hillside or rough, uneven terrain. They can be custom-fit to almost any area and be any size or shape. Decks can even be built around existing trees and other landmarks. Patios are another of the most flexible and convenient ways to enhance an outdoor living space. Plants and flowers help make these outdoor spaces more comfortable.

Porches, patios and decks create a comfortable, convenient place to relax and enjoy the outdoors. Benches, arbors, stairways and railings create the structural framework, while the natural beauty of the surrounding trees, shrubs, plants and flowers softens and enhances the entire setting. Shrubs, trees, fences or screens keep these outdoor rooms secluded and hidden from the view of neighbors.

Photo courtesy of Sticks and Stones Innovative Decks and Landscape Design

*(above) **An elaborate front yard landscape** greets visitors in grand style. As you approach the house, a circular brick patio creates a sunburst effect, which emanates from a small round planting area in the center. Leading from the patio to the house, a large cement bridge guides people over a small garden pond to the front entry of the house. Wide, low benches on either side of the bridge act as safety rails and offer ample seating for enjoying this attractive front yard area.*

This traditional porch stretches across the back of the house, offering a comfortable place to sit and a vantage point from which to view the backyard scenery.

PORCHES, PATIOS & DECKS

Patios are perfect for people who want low-maintenance landscapes for their yards. A patio can consist of a simple concrete pad, accessorized with a picnic table and some potted plants, or it can be an elaborate courtyard, complete with designer furniture, a theme garden and a pond.

(above) **A simple brick patio** *is the center of this delightful backyard garden. Red zinnias and geraniums add a burst of color to the lush landscape that encloses the patio area.*

(right) **A diamond-shaped planting area** *is the centerpiece of the patio in this formal backyard garden. An interesting combination of geometric shapes and colors, in both the patio design and the landscaping, paints a stunning outdoor picture.*

Irregular flagging stone is used for the patio and steps of this backyard area. The shape of the stone makes it easy to create open planting areas, such as the ones shown here, within the patio itself.

Photo courtesy of Bachman's Landscaping Service

PORCHES, PATIOS & DECKS

(above) **Creative use of landscape design** and *architecture helps turn a small backyard with a steep hill into a beautiful outdoor oasis. A small deck at the bottom of the hill offers a place to sit and enjoy the surroundings.*

(right) **Paper lanterns and candles** *are easy-to-make outdoor lighting options when you need lighting for the deck at the spur of the moment.*

Photo courtesy of Cy DeCosse Inc.

A large wooden pergola frames the doorway that leads from inside the house to the outdoor deck area. The open lattice design helps keep the hot sun from heating the inside of the house; the open-weave design also matches other design elements on the deck.

Managing Movement
PATHS & WALKWAYS

The elements you include as part of your landscape, and the places you put them, will dictate the way traffic flows through the entire area. In other words, landscape structures and elements such as steps, pathways, stairways, arbors, pergolas and gazebos guide garden users as they wander through the area. These elements make uneven terrain easier to walk over, and direct foot traffic from one part of the garden to another.

Elements like paths, walkways, steps and stairways all serve to link various areas of the yard. By using the same materials and design style used in other elements throughout the landscape, they help integrate the different areas into one harmonious setting. Walkways have two different purposes; they are either designed to get you to where you're going the quickest and most efficient way possible, or they are designed to help you slow down and literally smell the roses. Curved walkways keep users down to a stroll and can be used to create surprises, because not all of the garden can be seen at once. They provide an informal introduction to a garden.

If you need a walkway for heavy traffic or carrying large packages, a straight walk is more practical. Straight walks give a more linear and formal look to an outdoor area.

Paths and walkways can be both attractive and functional. They should be wide enough to allow two adults to walk side-by-side comfortably, and have a surface that provides secure footing in all kinds of weather. Walkways are generally wide and paved, while pathways are narrower and not paved. Use a mulch, such as bark chips, to create a woodland atmosphere that's suited for a pathway through a garden.

Photo courtesy of TCT Landscaping

Light-colored flagstone contrasts against the dark green lawn creating a system of pathways throughout this backyard setting. The pathway takes garden users from one area of interest to another, from a small garden pond to a separate flower garden and beyond.

Photo courtesy of Hanover Architectural Products

Exciting new shapes in brick pavers open new design opportunities to the landscape designer. The curved cut of the pavers and the winding design of the path create the illusion of a snake when viewed from above.

Large cement slabs *create a wide-open walkway around this formal garden setting. Flagstone is used to separate the cement slabs and add an interesting texture. Decorative outdoor furniture invites users to sit and enjoy the setting.*

BRIDGES & STEPS

Bridges, steps, and pathways should be designed and constructed to blend in with other elements in the landscape. They can even be painted in colors that match other structural elements, or in colors that are echoed in the natural garden surroundings.

Steps and pathways link one part of the garden with another, such as the transition between an open, sunny lawn and a shady woodland area. And bridges don't always have to cross water—some bridges create a pathway over a gap or gully, while others create the illusion of water by simply being placed over a location such as a dry creek bed.

Garden steps are used to connect different levels of a yard. The design and materials used should harmonize with other materials used throughout the landscape, especially with the walkways and paths they will be connecting. Garden steps should be comfortable and stable, and can be constructed from a number of materials, from natural stone to concrete to railroad ties. The type of material used will determine what kind of impact the steps will have on a landscape.

Brick, concrete, flagstone, tile and wood each bring a different feeling to a setting. Brick and stone have a more formal look, while loose aggregates and wood add a casual, informal feel to a landscape.

Brick and natural stone are popular choices for steps because they add warmth, color, pattern and texture to even the simplest landscapes. They offer a large selection of colors, textures, sizes and patterns to choose from, and are an easy choice for do-it-yourselfers.

A combination of natural stones was used to create interesting color contrasts within this lovely landscape.

A bright red foot bridge enhances the oriental motif of this outdoor setting. The bridge not only carries people over the small creek, it encourages movement from one part of the garden to another.

(above) **A cobblestone walkway** leads garden users over an arched wooden bridge, that spans a small creek, and into a cozy woodland area of this yard.

(left) **Large slabs of fieldstone** were used within this pathway to make wide steps that guide people safely down a slight hill and around a corner.

(above) **Delightful brass spouting fish sculptures** *add an enchanting accent to this water garden. (inset photo)* **This large pond** *displays a variety of the different types of water plants, such as submerged, floating and emergent (bog plants). Large boulders create a natural cascade of water and a beautiful surrounding for this wonderful water garden.*

42

Types of Gardens
GREAT GARDEN IDEAS

Because gardening is a highly personalized art, two different gardeners will give two identical pieces of land very different looks after they have finished with them. For your personal landscape garden you can choose from a variety of garden types, such as water gardens, herb gardens, flower gardens, shade gardens, and sculpture gardens, just to name a few. Even shrubs and hedges serve to create privacy as well as add a fragrant scent to the air.

Any type of garden can be incorporated into a landscape without compromising any other areas. Even a small yard or urban apartment can include some kind of garden. No matter what type, a garden should be personal and comfortable to the owner, be it a condo deck with potted plants, a formal manicured courtyard or a suburban lot turned into the Garden of Eden.

Lush green environments and colorful garden settings give a romantic tone to a backyard setting. A garden that is made up of curves creates a more romantic effect. The straight lines of the landscape, such as walls, steps or other structural elements, should be planted with lush, flowering growth that softens the hard edges by flowing over them.

Gardens are also popular settings for displaying statues and sculpture. Display niches can be created among the greenery to display sculptures or they can be made the center of attention in a courtyard garden. Statues are often used in fountains or at the entrance to the garden, like sentinels.

Adding color, shape and texture, in the form of flowers and shrubs, are other ways to create interesting visual effects.

Photo courtesy of Cy DeCosse Inc.

This picturesque landscape is the perfect example of what proper planning and a love of landscape gardening can create. This landscape uses colorful flower gardens to paint a breathtaking portrait in this backyard. Manicured shrubs add an interesting effect and draw attention to the circular patio sitting area.

Types of Gardens
FLOWER GARDENS

Flower gardens, such as annual, perennial and bulb gardens, can also be considered a type of collection used for display in a theme garden. They can grouped by a particular plant family, such as ferns or roses, or according to common features, such as color. An example might be an all-white, or a blue-and-white garden. The type of light and quality of soil conditions will also determine what types of plants are best suited for the different areas of your landscape garden. Pale-colored blooms look best in the soft light of shaded areas. These lighter colors look washed-out in bright sunlight. Hot colors like red and fuchsia are ideal for sunny spots, as well as areas like water gardens, where you'd like an exotic effect.

Annuals are plants that last for only one growing season. These types of plants produce some of the most brilliant flowers of any plants. They create instant color in a container garden, window box or planter, and you can mix annuals with perennials to ensure color throughout the blooming season.

Perennials will flower every year after the first year they bloom. For most perennials the flowers only last for about three weeks. You can plant perennials in stages to coordinate the blooming periods and have constant color all season long. Bulbs are perennials that can be forced indoors to create a bloom at any time of year.

The most effective flower gardens require careful plant selection, such as spring-flowering and summer-flowering types, as well as thoughtful blending of colors, textures and shapes of plants.

Informal wild flower gardens will succeed if the flowers are indigenous, or well adapted, to your regional area.

This versatile garden designed with fast-growing perennials and showy annuals is a natural for any sunny area in the landscape. A quick sunny garden like this is an excellent way to add bright color from spring to late fall.

Plant a stunning display of annuals and perennials by interplanting different varieties. Choose plants with varying heights and plant them where they won't block the view from the porch. This vibrant mix of colors and textures includes French marigolds, daises and sweet alyssum.

SHADE & VEGETABLE GARDENS

Although there are many flowering plants that tolerate shade, many types of shade-loving plants, such as impatiens, will grow spindly in deep shade. Constant light shade, or deep shade for only a portion of the day, is tolerable for most shade gardens.

Dense tree shade and high walls are the most difficult shade problems to overcome. Tree shade is easily remedied by removing a few branches, while walls are not so easily removed. Painting the base of the wall a light color and using white limestone chips as ground cover can increase the amount of light in the garden. The mirrorlike calmness of a pond or pool can also reflect light into a shaded area of the garden.

Growing your own food is both fun and satisfying. Whether you garden in expansive beds or small containers, vegetables, fruits and herbs that you grow yourself are fresher and better-tasting than those sold at the grocery store.

Many edible plants can be attractive additions to a flower garden as well. Herbs are often planted for their fragrance and interesting texture, and small fruit trees, such as crab apples, for their colorful spring blossoms.

Vegetables and flowers can be mixed together with great success. In fact, mixing flowers and vegetables in a garden has a number of advantages, such as using strong-scented plants like marigolds or garlic to repel insects that feed on vegetables. For a clever twist, include vegetables, such as ornamental cabbage, in flower beds, or plant a row of tall-growing flowers as a decorative, natural fence around your vegetable plot.

Ornamental cabbage is planted among traditional annuals and perennials for a unique effect. Different forms of ornamental cabbage or a single plant can make a dramatic accent. This ornamental vegetable holds its color through the fall and, in northern regions, these plants stand out against the white snow.

Photos, both pages, courtesy of Cy DeCosse Inc.

(above) **A variety of hostas** are mixed with other shade-loving plants to create an attractive border garden. The neat, compact form of hostas makes them a striking plant to use to define garden spaces and outline garden pathways.

(left) **A small border garden** aligns this rustic fence and softens the transition from the fence to the ground. Shade-loving plants in varying shades of purple, and interesting shapes and textures make this a charming little accent in the yard.

47

Types of Gardens

CONTAINER & SCULPTURE GARDENS

Planting in containers lets you extend the beauty of the garden beyond its traditional boundaries to areas that would otherwise be bare. Container plantings can also be moved and rearranged fairly easily, and having this flexibility can make container gardening particularly enjoyable. Windowsills, stairways and rooftops are just a few of the spots where container gardens can dramatically change and enhance the look and feel of a space.

Gardens have always been a showcase for durable art such as sculpture. There are two ways to approach a sculpture garden design. One is to display the statues in plain surroundings as the centerpiece of the garden. The other is to surround the sculpture with plants.

The majestic beauty and size of the crane is captured in these bronze fountains. Their classic old-world charm brings elegance to the garden.

Photo courtesy of The Brass Baron

(left) **Punctuate your garden** with a contrasting element that gently surprises the viewer, such as this child's wagon. Unusual objects can become attractive containers as long as they have adequate drainage.

(bottom left) **Decorative containers,** filled with colorful flowers, carry the formal theme of this front yard landscape. Chrysanthemums in pots are sold in bloom throughout the summer and fall and will instantly brighten a bare garden area.

(bottom right) **An old-fashioned sundial statue** becomes a focal point in this garden. The statue, almost buried in the foliage, is located where it will surprise and charm those passing by.

49

A PORTFOLIO OF
WATER GARDEN & SPECIALTY LANDSCAPE IDEAS

WATER GARDENS

Combining water, stone and vegetation is a time-tested way to create a peaceful, relaxing atmosphere. The reflection of the sky, clouds or landscape on a pool offers a beautiful and ever-changing spectacle. A full-scale traditional reflecting pool may be impractical for most people, but modern landscaping takes space and cost into account and provides homeowners with many water garden and pool options.

Adapt the pool style to the surrounding environment or architecture. For instance, classic rectangular or oval shapes with sculpture or fountains recall Victorian pools from years ago. These pools look best when surrounded by a neat, well-groomed landscape.

Natural pools give the appearance of small ponds. These pools have no corners or perpendicular walls and generally feature native stone and vegetation.

Small accent pools can be simple as a birdbath or intricate as a garden path fountain. These pools are usually featured in a garden or along a path to provide diversity to the ear and the eye.

No matter its size, shape or style, remember that by building a pool you are creating a true ecosystem in your own backyard. For many people, a decorative pool becomes a full-scale hobby with large, multicolored carp, or koi, stocked as pets. However, be prepared for nightly visits from local wildlife, and design the water garden with the natural environment in mind. Keep the water clean and pure with good aeration, and stock it with indigenous, oxygenating plants.

Create a garden environment that meets your needs, yet seems completely natural and serene. By planting your favorite water-loving vegetation, you can customize a water garden to your personal tastes.

(right) **For a more cultured look,** *create a traditional water garden with sculpture and paved walkways. Traditional water gardens generally require more effort to maintain, but their benefits are obvious.*

(below) **With the right combination** *of stone, flowers and water, you can create small areas of natural beauty in your own backyard.*

Photos both pages courtesy of Lilypons Water Gardens

Unremarkable areas are transformed into unforgettable scenes with a well-planned water garden. The sight and sounds of flowing water, framed by the splendor of nature, have a tranquil, soothing effect. Whether your plans involve huge, awe-inspiring reflection pools or subtle backyard ponds, you can count on the beauty and tranquilty of a tasteful water garden.

(below) *A few scattered boulders* provide texture and diversity to the water garden environment. The spray from a fountain glistens brightly on the rocks to create a natural sparkle and brightness in the area.

Photo courtesy of Featherock, Incorporated

With the right resources, *you can create a scene that is staggeringly beautiful. This pool was designed in the natural style and is framed by boulders and stone to form a private oasis with unobtrusive boundaries.*

Many people want their water gardens to harbor the pure features of wildlife. Indigenous vegetation and local stone can make even an artificial pond appear as an extension of the surrounding landscape. These small water sources attract nearby wildlife, from birds to raccoons, to make the area a true facet of the ecosystem. In this way, water gardens become more than visual features of your property; they allow you to connect with nature and enjoy the beauty it offers.

Photo courtesy of Claudia Hodges/Waterscapes

*A **small pond** can be expanded with small features. Stocking the pond with fish and water plants makes the whole setting more enjoyable.*

(left) **Cattails and lily pads** make an artificial pond appear as a wooded watering hole to create a feeling of untouched beauty.

(below) **Lush background greenery** emphasizes the bright colors of the flowering vegetation. Planning the garden vegetation is an important part of the design process.

Photos this page courtesy of Lilypons Water Gardens

Photo courtesy of Mee Industries Inc

Paved walkways, *trimmed vegetation and gentle, curving lines make this water garden a subtle and sophisticated backyard feature.*

(left) *A tiny pond* helped to transform a neglected field into enjoyable recreational space. It complements and provides perspective to a view of the wide horizon.

(below) *Stocking koi* in your water garden can become a true hobby. With a little patience and time, these remarkable fish can be trained to feed from your hand, and even surface when called.

(right) **A small pond enhances the beauty** *of a well-groomed yard. The local stone and vegetation add to the natural appearance of the pond.*

(below) **For breathtaking color** *in your water garden, plant large numbers of blooming plants that thrive in a damp environment.*

THEME GARDENS

Like a room in your home, a garden can adopt certain themes or patterns. From the type of vegetation used, to the layout and design of the area, the garden is a versatile and powerful creative outlet. Just as in an interior room, the lighting and space must be taken into account.

Try to build a particular mood with your garden. What plants you choose, and how you place them, can have an important effect on the overall look of the garden. Experiment with plant choices to create just the right color combination. In addition to the visual concerns, remember that different types of vegetation have very different water and sunlight needs.

Many people prefer to organize their garden along a distinct style. Chinese gardens, for example, emphasize dramatic rocks, trickling water and close-pruned shrubs. Indian gardens have geometrical layouts and are filled with square and rectangular shapes. They also frequently feature reflecting pools and fountains. Italian renaissance gardens generally feature steep hillsides with steps and terraces. Gardens such as these are, unlike flower gardens, stylistically difficult to mix. If you favor a particular theme, it's best to keep the concept fairly pure.

When doing your initial planning, remember that a garden can be organized according to any number of specialized characteristics. Some gardens are designed to look great in the moonlight; others are made to attract colorful butterflies. The choice is completely up to you.

Create strips of color *with a well-planned flower garden. In addition to color strategies, you should also carefully plan the size and shape of the garden area.*

(below) **The beauty** of a delicate flower can be touching in its pure simplicity. This hybrid rose combines the best features of parent species to create a more attractive flower.

Small gardens, or a simple cluster of flowers, can disguise or obscure unwanted yard features. Here an unsightly fence is shrouded by tall flowering plants.

The garden itself becomes a wall to border the property and create an element of privacy in this backyard. Unlike an artifical fence, a garden fence can create enclosure without hard confining lines.

(right) ***A narrow garden*** *with eye-catching boulders casts a bit of visual diversity upon an otherwise unremarkable yard environment.*

(below) ***The unusual shape and beauty of*** *gladiolus makes it a favorite in backyard gardens.*

(above) **The size and shape of the vegetation** *were clearly taken into account when this garden was planned. The plants in back provide a flat green background for the shorter, more colorful flowers in front.*

(right) **The diversity of colored flowers** *available to the home gardener is nearly endless. Choose from striking red or simple white, and transform your garden into a natural painter's canvas.*

Photos both pages courtesy of Cy DeCosse Inc.

Sometimes a little color *is all that's needed to turn a dull yard into an interesting, ever-changing scene. A splattering of bright color works wonders on a small patch of grass.*

(right) **In dry environments**, *landscaping can be more difficult, but even a desert environment can support a beautiful garden. These flowering cacti thrive in arid desert lands.*

Photos both pages courtesy of TCT Landscaping

(below) **This back-yard cactus garden** showcases the beauty of the vegetation. The plants grow low to the ground, as if hiding from the dry, pounding heat of the desert.

BACKYARD SANCTUARY

In today's world, privacy is getting hard to come by. In order to fully enjoy their yard and free time, many people need a secure, sheltered area, free from public distractions like noise and traffic. There are several landscaping methods you can use to transform your yard from an open, exposed area to a private, secure oasis. Consider your options carefully. Of course, how you decide to make your backyard sanctuary is dependent on space and cost, but consider the long-range effects of the landscaping changes. These types of landscaping changes can be major projects, but if you value your privacy, you'll find they are well worth the work.

If you are working with a small area, consider simply putting in a fence or a wall for privacy.

Fences and walls shelter the area while taking up a minimum of space, and offer an increased level of security and protection. If you are concerned about obtrusive-looking walls or fences, use vines, trees or hedges to temper the hard edges and corners. However, fences can be designed with structural originality to become attractive yard features, rather than a utilitarian shield. Other structures like gazebos or trellises can also muffle noise and shelter your activities from prying eyes. Vegetation itself can serve as a shield for your lawn. Hedges, trees and vines are natural and effective barriers. Consider double or even triple rows of shrubs or clipped hedges when using vegetation as a visual barrier.

Creativity can be the key with any outdoor design. An unusual bench design adds a special style to this backyard sanctuary.

Many times the slope of your lawn determines the amount of privacy you get. A bare, overly flat yard seems more open and public than a hilly, wooded nook. Landscape the lawn to include berms, hills or gradual slopes to vary the scene and provide diversity to the visual image.

Photos this page courtesy of California Redwood Association

(above) **Trees and vines** *help to provide cover, making the fence seem like a mere portion of this yard's barrier to the outside world.*

(right) **Well-groomed shrubs** *and curling shade trees provide texture and depth to temper the flat appearance of a slatted fence.*

The location *of a favorite piece of lawn furniture is important to the private enjoyment of the yard. This bench seems sequestered in a niche framed by boulders and a background of shrubs.*

77

(right) **Nature creates all the landscaping anyone** *could want, with tall trees framing a staggering view of the lake.*

(right) **Lush greenery** *in the background provides a striking contrast to the refined gazebo and flower bed in the main yard.*

Photo courtesy of Claudia Hodges/ Waterscapes

The feeling of nature in the city is achieved in this backyard courtyard. The screened porch shields the yard from prying eyes, while the creeping ground vines make the area a truly secluded sanctuary.

The garden and house mesh on this backyard veranda. The vines and plants encroach upon the patio tile to bring nature just a little closer to home.

(right) **Create landscaping designs** *that favor comfortable observation. This gazebo allows you to enjoy the bordering vegetation while keeping an eye on the pool.*

(below) **Small berms add texture to the front yard** *and raise the planting platform for small shrubs and trees. Inventive strategies such as these make landscaping a creative activity, while increasing the level of privacy.*

Photo courtesy of Bachman's Landscaping Service

VISUAL IMPRESSIONS

More than in the home, the garden and yard present you with the opportunity to experiment with visual impressions. If the area is cramped, you can use several methods to "trick" the eye into seeing more space. Colorful flowers in the foreground, sitting in contrast to background greenery, create the feeling of depth. Just as in painting, tapered lines and multilayered scenes affect the perspective.

Overhead structures can be comforting oases in a disordered universe. Large areas can be subdivided into more intimate sections, separated by shrubs or walls. Draw attention to important features with good outdoor lighting, or by arranging the area in such a way as to focus the attention. Carefully placed garden decorations draw the gaze by sheer virtue of their location.

Texture can be the key when trying to create the illusion of space. Terraces create level activity areas on sloping land, while stairways allow you to easily gain access to areas all along a sloping hillside.

When planting your garden vegetation, remember to take into account the height of each plant species. Keeping the flower levels relatively even creates the image of a flowing, vibrant sea of color, while a more uneven distribution might offer more of a layered approach to home landscape design.

Row after row of color and texture gives you a visually pleasing image while drawing the eye into the background and sky. This multi-layered strategy creates an image of space and openess.

(right) **A flowering sea of vegetation** *erupts in contrast to the well-trimmed yard surrounding the flower patch.*

(below) **A rainbow of color** *seems to explode from the ground. For most people, the sheer brightness found in nature makes the care and effort of gardening well worth it.*

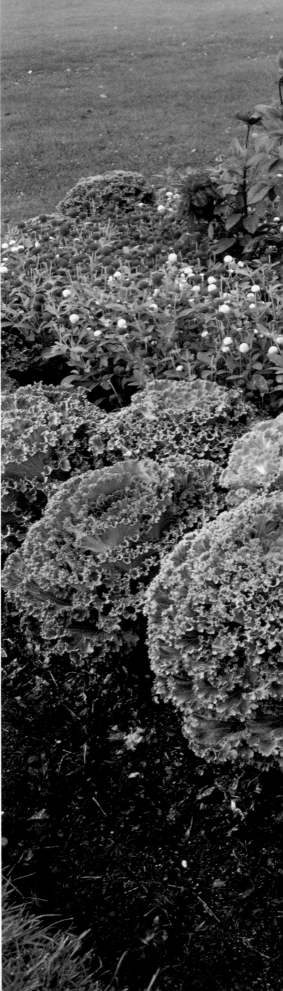

Photos both pages courtesy of Cy DeCosse Inc.

(left) **The incredibly diverse vegetation** in this yard stands out at night, when a few well-placed lights highlight the low-lying flowers and spiraling trees along the porch.

(below) **A yard light brings out the best** in this potted plant. The light casts interesting shadows in the background and forms a deep reflection in the small garden pool.

(right) **Small ground lights around the garden** help to create the illusion of space by flowing along the borders and illuminating the entire yard.

(below) **With a few wooden lanterns** a backyard forest becomes a natural walking garden complete with pathways. The shape of the lanterns adds to the romantic, almost fanciful atmosphere of the setting.

Photo courtesy of Idaho Wood

(right) **Layered rock construction** combines with flowing water and deep shrubbery to create a stunning natural environment.

(below) **The overhead construction** of an Oriental trellis, combined with a string of lights, gives a backyard depth and texture.

Photo courtesy of Cy DeCosse Inc.

Photo courtesy of Intermatic Incorporated

PORTFOLIO

(right) **Retaining walls allow you** to take advantage of unused space and make the yard seem just a little more striking and dramatic.

(below) **A formal front yard landscape** greets callers to this stunning estate. The formal walkway leading to the front door follows a beautifully planted flagstone retaining wall. A brook lined with natural stone gives the effect of a moat as it winds its way around the house.

Photo courtesy of Charles Cudd Co., Chuck Carver Photography, Mpls., both photos courtesy of Buechel Stone Corp of Chilton and Fon du lac, Wisconsin.

LIST OF CONTRIBUTORS

We'd like to thank the following companies for providing the photographs used in this book:

Anchor Wall Systems
6101 Baker Road, Suite 201
Minnetonka, MN 55345
(612) 933-8855
Anchor Diamond®, Anchor Windsor Stone®,
& Anchor Sahara Stone® retaining wall
systems are nationally available at better
home centers.

Bachman's Landscaping Service
6010 Lyndale Avenue South
Minneapolis, MN 55419
(612) 861-7600

The Brass Baron
10151 Pacific Mesa Blvd., Suite 104
San Diego, CA 92121
(800) 536-0987

Bow Bends
P.O. Box 900
Bolton, MA 01740
(508) 779-6464

Buechel Stone Corp.
W3639 Hwy H
Chilton, WI 53014
(414) 849-9361

California Redwood Association
405 Enfrente Drive, Suite 200
Novato, CA 94949
(415) 382-0662

Champlain Stone, Ltd.
P.O. Box 650
Warrensburg, NY 12885
(518) 623-2902
fax (518) 623-3088

CROSS VINYLattice
3174 Marian Drive
Atlanta, GA 30340
(770) 451-4531

Featherock, Inc.
United States Pumice Co.
20219 Bahama Street
Chatsworth, CA 91311
(800) 423-3037

Gardenside, Ltd.
999 Andersen Drive, Suite 140
San Rafael, CA 94901
phone: (415) 455-4500
fax: (415) 455-4505

Gazebo Central
1000 Ken-O-Sha Ind. Dr. S.E.
Grand Rapids, MI 49508
(800) 339-0288

Hanover Architectural Products
240 Bender Road
Hanover, PA 17331
(717) 637-0500

Hanover Lantern
470 High Street
Hanover PA 17331
(717) 632-6464

Idaho Wood
P.O. Box 488
Sandpoint, ID 83864
(800) 635-1100

Intermatic, Inc.
Intermatic Plaza
Spring Grove, IL 60081-9698
(815) 675-2321

Keystone Retaining Wall Systems, Inc.
4444 West 78th Street
Minneapolis, MN 55435
(612) 897-1040

Lilypons Water Gardens
7000 Lilypons Road
Buckeystown, MD 21717
(301) 874-5503

Lindal Cedar Homes, Inc.
P.O. Box 24426
Seattle, WA 98124
(206) 725-0900

Mee Industries Inc.
4443 North Rowland Avenue
El Monte, CA 91731
(818) 350-4180

Milt Charno & Associates
611 North Mayfair Road
Wauwatosa, WI 53226
(414) 475-1965

Noral Lighting, a division of Hydrel
12881 Bradley Avenue
Sylmar, CA 91342
(818) 362-9465

Otterbine Barebo, Inc.
3840 Main Road East
Emmaus, PA 18049
(800) 237-8837

Sticks and Stones Innovative Decks
and Landscape Design
2822 West 43rd Street
Minneapolis, MN 55410
(612) 920-2400

TCT Landscaping
P.O. Box 1218
Solvang, CA 93464
(805) 688-3741

TetraPond
3001 Commerce Street
Blacksburg, VA 24060
(540) 951-5400

VERSA-LOK Retaining
Wall Systems
P.O. Box 9220
North St. Paul, MN 55109
(800) 770-4525

Waterscapes/Claudia Hodges
5520 Little River Circle
Gainesville, GA 30506
(770) 536-7282

Weatherend Estate Furniture
6 Gordon Drive
Rockland, ME 04841
(207) 596-6483

Weyerhaeuser
P.O. Box 189
R.D. #2, Campbell Road
Titusville, PA 16354
(800) 723-1012